INNER LIGHT

An Oracle Book of
Guidance & Affirmations

TONI CARMINE SALERNO

BLUE ANGEL®
PUBLISHING

Inner Light

Published by Blue Angel Publishing
80 Glen Tower Drive, Glen Waverley,
Victoria, Australia 3150
E-mail: info@blueangelonline.com
Website: www.blueangelonline.com

Artwork and text by Toni Carmine Salerno
Edited by Danielle Taylor & Tanya Graham

Blue Angel is a registered trademark of Blue Angel Gallery Pty. Ltd.

ISBN: 978-1-922161-43-7

Introduction

May this book inspire you to look within. You can use it as an oracle by opening it randomly at any page, or you can initially read it through to the end if you prefer. My hope is that it will help you to view your life from a higher spiritual perspective, and also help you to become more aware of your true spiritual and creative nature, which is unlimited and transcends both time and space.

One of my guiding principles is that we are all essentially energy; an intelligent creative energy through which all is interconnected. There are many names given to this energy, but regardless of the name we give it, I think we are all referring to the same thing; a universal force which stems from the very heart of all creation. In this book I refer to it as "inner light." It exists within me and you and every blade of grass. It is in the air, the trees, the oceans and streams. It is within sunlight, in the stars, earth and sky, and even exists within darkness.

This inner light however, is visible only through our inner vision. It is a light that understands us, but cannot be understood by us because, for the time being at least, it is beyond our capacity to understand it. It can be felt, it can be sensed, it can guide us and give us hope and comfort, but only if we have faith, only if we trust, only if we are open-hearted and open-minded.

This little book is not here to connect you with your inner light for you are already connected. It is simply here to remind you to look within and discover that you are so much more than you have been told you are. Your inner light is your true nature. It is not your body, it is not your mind, it is the true and eternal you.

With love and eternal blessings,
Toni Carmine Salerno

*

About Positive Affirmations

A positive affirmation is a statement which, when repeated often, can help transform our negative thoughts and attitudes. Affirmations essentially reprogram the mind and they transform and empower us. All it takes is a little commitment, patience and perseverance.

Each message in this book is followed by a set of positive affirmations. You can repeat these out loud or silently. The important thing is that you own each word. Be fully present with the words and feel them resonate inside you. At first the process can seem strange. Your mind will question whether what you are saying is even possible. This is completely normal. It is the mind's job to question everything, so don't be put off by this. Practice and repeat your affirmations anyway, as the more you do, the more they will become part of you. What you affirm will come to be.

*

Creating Your Own Affirmations

Once you become familiar with using affirmations you can create your own. The affirmations in this book are only a starting point. Here are a few tips on making your own affirmations. Try to avoid using words like no, not, should, won't or haven't. Make every statement positive and always affirm in the present tense. For example, "I am wealthy," "I am joyful," and "I am creative" work better than "I will be wealthy," "I will be joyful," and "I will be creative."

When repeated often, these affirmations will become part of you and trigger positive thoughts, attitudes, responses and actions. Words can either help to build or destroy. Positive affirmations can be building blocks to help you build the life of your dreams.

I Am Blessed

"The way is perfect like vast space where nothing is lacking and nothing is in excess."
– Sosan

A natural balance exists in our world. Through the universal principle of complimentary opposites known as Yin and Yang and the Law of Cause and Effect, life is kept in perfect balance. The present circumstance is steering you to the centre, back to balance, back to something greater. There is a blessing here but perhaps it is not visible at this moment. In time something beautiful manifests. Surrender feelings of resentment or frustration. Trust that all is unfolding in the most perfect way for you and those around you. Plant seeds of faith and love and you will reap a blessed harvest.

Affirmation
All is unfolding in the most perfect way for me and others.
All unfolds in perfect time.
I am blessed with eternal love and life.

I Am Truth

Not speaking your truth may cause more harm than good.
Let your true feelings be known. Express yourself clearly.
Courage is essential, especially now. A heavy weight is lifted from
your shoulders.

Know that the truth, when spoken honestly and lovingly, does
not really hurt anyone. There may initially be hurt feelings,
disappointment or anger but this soon dissolves. The truth sets
you and others free.

Affirmation
In my heart lies my truth.
I express myself clearly, honestly and lovingly.
I am courageous and move through life with ease and harmony.

Transformation

You are engaged in negative thinking and self-criticism due to a diminished sense of self-worth. See the beauty within and around you. Stop judging the qualities you don't like about yourself as 'bad' – this is simply an illusion. You are filled with endless potential. Love is your true nature.

Life is made up of complimentary parts. Sometimes these are called 'opposites,' but they are not really opposites because they are inseparable. You cannot have good without bad, love without hate, or happy without sad, as they are joined together.

Life is always flowing from one side to the other. Opposites are two sides of the same coin but they are also connected, they are touching, they are one. In rejecting parts of yourself, you also reject a part of life. Accept yourself as you are. Make no distinction. There is nothing to change except your perceptions. Love and accept all as it is and all transforms.

Affirmation
I love, embrace and accept every part of me.
I see and feel the beauty within me.
I love and accept the world as it is.
There is nothing that I need to change; there is only love.

Wings of Light

A beautiful angel full of light and love stands before you.
She wants you to know that you are dearly loved, more than you
can possibly ever imagine. Even though you feel lonely at times,
know that you are never truly alone.

Close your eyes right now and feel a divine presence, your divine
presence. Feel unconditional love flow in and out of your being.
Imagine it as a multi-coloured stream of light. Breathe in this
light of unconditional love, as it ebbs and flows in the ocean of
your being, and gently breathe it out.

Affirmation
I am the light of unconditional love.
I breathe in love and breathe out light.
Only love surrounds me.
I am loved. I am love.

The Way

All obstacles have vanished and your time of waiting is over. The challenges you have faced were essential to your ultimate success but now you can move forward with confidence and clarity. The way is finally clear.

Sometimes we must wait until the timing is right. Just as nature has her seasons, so too do you move through your own cycles. Accept and respect life's natural rhythms and know there is a time to move forward, and a time to be still.

Affirmation
I am one with life.
All manifests at the most perfect time.
I am guided by a loving Universe.
I now move forward with ease.

Joy

Take a moment to reflect and be grateful for every experience
and know that all has served a purpose in your life.
You deserve to be and have all that your heart truly desires.
Listen to your heart and follow its wisdom. You will intuitively
know which path to follow.

When things feel right it is a confirmation from the Universe
that you are following the call of your heart. Allow yourself to be
still and acknowledge this moment, this life, this breath, and the
joy that resides inside you. It may not always seem so, but deep
inside you an eternal flame glows and life is always beautiful.

Affirmation
I celebrate and feel the joy of life.
I love and appreciate each moment.
I am an eternal flame of love.

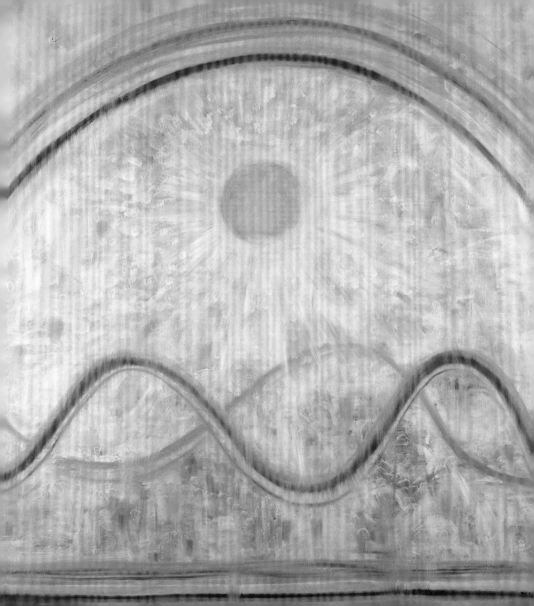

Eternal Soul

You are a radiant being, full of love and light, innate wisdom and knowledge. Look clearly with the eyes of love and you will see this is true. You have so many beautiful qualities, and yet you often have a distorted view.

I am here to help you reconnect with the infinite creative power you hold within.

Close your eyes and focus on your breath. Imagine breathing in and breathing out healing golden light. Breathe light into your heart and every part of your body. Let light flow into your thoughts and emotions. This is the light of unconditional love, the divine light of your soul that stems from eternity, and loves you eternally.

Affirmation
I am the light of love.
My soul is infinite and eternal.
I hold infinite creative power.

The Golden Glow

Life is a warm golden glow that flows out from you, expanding endlessly in every direction. Your life is essentially a journey upon a path of love.

You are a radiant being of light, made up of every colour of the rainbow, flowing out to infinity. You are vast space, the horizon, the sun, a river flowing to an infinite sea of love.

Your soul is the golden path you travel, and the breeze is the guiding flow of your spirit.

Affirmation
I travel the golden path of my soul's infinite light.
The way is clear like the vastness of space.
My inner light expands in every direction.
I am one with all of creation.

Heart and Soul

Let go of logic and trust your inner feelings and intuition. Pay attention to what you feel. What is your heart saying? Don't try to think of the answer, rather allow it to surface from inside you. The heart is the gateway to the soul. The way forward may be hidden, but trust your instincts and you will be intuitively guided and protected. Courage and faith are called for in this moment. All is possible when the heart and mind are in alignment. Trust in your intuition – your inner wisdom.

Affirmation
I listen to my heart and I am guided by its wisdom and love.
My heart and mind are in perfect alignment.
I have courage and faith in myself.

Inner Conflict

"The Great Way is not difficult for those who have no preferences. When love and hate are both absent everything becomes clear and undisguised. Make the smallest distinction, however, and heaven and earth are set infinitely apart. If you wish to see the truth then hold no opinion for or against. The struggle of what one likes and what one dislikes is the disease of the mind."
– Sosan

We are taught to accept or reject things, labelling them as either good or bad. This act of choosing creates an inner conflict as it divides and separates, and we only see one side or the other but never the whole picture.

We want others to see the parts of us that we think are good and lovable and we try to hide the aspects of ourselves that we perceive to be bad and unlovable. In doing this we fail to see that every part of us is a necessary piece of the whole; every part equally valuable and worthy of love.

To feel whole one must love and embrace every aspect of oneself without distinction, and have no preference either for, or against.

Affirmation
I accept and love myself.
Every part of me is lovable and worthy of love.
I make no distinction either for or against.

Believe

The Universe is testing your faith and resolve. This calls for courage, but know that you are supported by an infinite Universe of love. Stand firm in your beliefs regardless of what others may say or think.

Listen to your inner guidance and use your discernment to determine when you must stand your ground and when it is best to walk away.

Affirmation
*I stand firm in my beliefs while respecting the beliefs of others.
I am supported by a loving and benevolent Universe.*

Imagination

"Logic will get you from A to B.
Imagination will take you everywhere."
– Albert Einstein

Tapping into your imagination and creativity unleashes new possibilities. Surrender to your inner urge to create and birth something new. With an open heart and mind, wonderful opportunities present themselves.

Think outside the square. Be playful and childlike in your approach, as your inner child is the true artist. Don't take things too seriously; this is a time for fun and exploration, which leads to an abundant and fulfilling future.

Spend time in nature and strengthen your connection with the earth. Feel her fertile and healing energy fuelling your imagination, and filling your heart with peace and love.

Affirmation
My imagination is infinite.
I am open to new and exciting possibilities.
My inner child is a brilliant artist.

The Eternal Moment

Someone is thinking of you this very moment and sending you their love.

Thoughts and feelings are living energies that float within the ocean of human consciousness, transcending both time and space. We are all energetically interconnected, all part of the world wide web of human consciousness. Know that your thoughts and feelings can be intuitively sensed by others, especially those you love or think of often.

If you are missing someone who has moved or passed away, know you are always spiritually connected to them. Feel their presence now. All that is united in love is eternal.

Affirmation
My love transcends space and time.
Everyone I love is present in my heart.
All is eternal and interconnected.

A New Beginning

A new chapter unfolds bringing a renewed sense of clarity and purpose.

Through serendipitous events you are intuitively guided to explore new places and possibilities. Embrace the new and let go of all that no longer serves a useful purpose in your life. The past is behind you, bless it, give thanks for all that has been and move on.

Life is forever flowing, changing and embracing ever-greater spheres of love and wisdom. Enjoy each moment, and be grateful for every blessing.

Affirmation
I am one with life's eternal flow.
I bless the past and embrace the power of now.
My life is full of new rich and rewarding experiences.

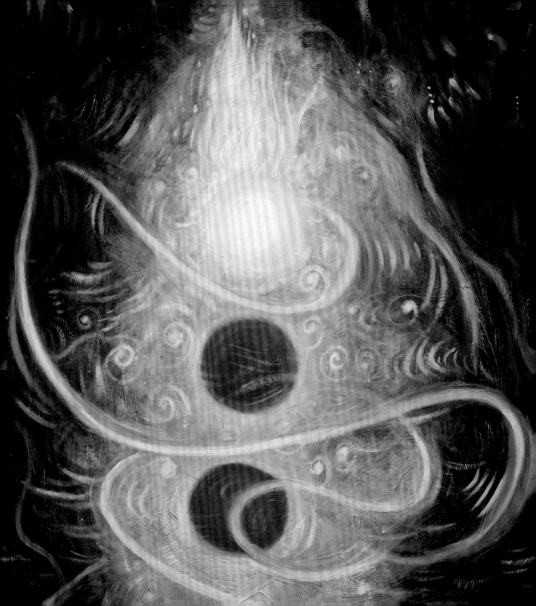

Change

It is time to trust and let go of old emotional ties and outmoded ways of thinking. Identify beliefs that no longer serve you, and free yourself from negative entanglements to clear the way for a positive future.

With patience and commitment comes success. New possibilities and inspirational change create wholeness. Change is coming in the form of a great blessing.

Affirmation
I invite blessed change into my life.
I am free of all negative entanglements.
I surrender the thoughts and feelings that no longer serve me,
and replace these with love.

The Golden Treasure

Cease all negative thinking and acknowledge your uniqueness and special qualities in this sacred moment.

The qualities you admire in others are also within you. Connect with the golden treasure that resides within you and it will be reflected outwards into your world. Know that an infinite supply of abundance will flow like a steady stream to you once your perceptions are balanced.

Affirmation
*I love and honour my uniqueness and my many special qualities.
Inside me is a golden treasure that flows an infinite supply of
abundance into my life.
My heart is a river of gold.*

A Ray of Sunlight

A bright new chapter in the story of your life is unfolding with the birth of something new.

Through the darkness of night we are able to see the beautiful tapestry of stars above us. Life can seem gloomy at times and it may be hard to see the light at the end of the tunnel. Know that through the darkness a light will always shine.

A ray of sunlight bursts through the clouds and the first buds of spring appear. Your whole world is about to blossom as all that has been dormant comes to life.

Affirmation
Every experience makes me wiser and stronger.
The rays of love always shine on me.
I embrace this new chapter of my life.

Heart Space

Dwelling on the past serves no purpose. Surrender to the whisper of an ethereal wind that blows and clears away negative feelings connected to the past. The way is now clear for new energies and possibilities to enter.

Close your eyes and feel a light in your heart centre. Breathe in the light and as you exhale, release all unwanted thoughts and feelings associated with the past, present or future. Continue to breathe in healing light, and breathe out all that is no longer worthy of you.

Immerse yourself in the crystal clear, vast peaceful space within you.

Affirmation
My heart and mind are clear.
There is infinite space and peace inside me.
My life is in perfect balance.
I fully embrace the present moment.

Blessing

Love and wellness flow to you and a blessing is on its way. Look below the surface and connect with the soul and spirit of all those around you. See only love in every heart and give and receive with an open heart.

Glance below the surface and connect with the soul and spirit of life. Life is a flowering blossom, a gift, a blessing.

Affirmation
Love and wellness flow to me.
I give and receive with an open heart in the spirit of love.
I am grateful for the blessings and abundance in my life.
I am blessed.

Perspective

An emotionally charged episode is soon to be healed or resolved.
An eruption. A release.

Now is also a time to listen and respect all points of view, for
everyone has their own perspective. From high above all is clear
but down below there is confusion. As the storm clears things
become clearer and a blessing is revealed.

Affirmation
I listen to and respect all points of view.
I look at things from a higher perspective.
I am blessed.

Unconditional Love

"Knowing others is wisdom, knowing yourself is enlightenment."
– Lao Tzu

This is a time of reflection and healing. Through our relationship with others, we learn more about ourselves. The purpose of all relationships is to help us grow our love, wisdom and compassion.

Our connections with others provide the perfect vehicle to support us in the lessons we need to learn. Through our relationships we come to realise that the judgements we make of others, are really judgements we make about ourselves. Relationships help us accept and broaden our understanding of life. They also serve as mirrors that reflect that which is wounded inside us and help us to heal.

Affirmation
I accept and love myself as I am.
I accept and love others as they are.

The Journey

"The journey of a thousand miles begins with one step."
– Lao Tzu

Don't be discouraged as setbacks can sometimes be a blessing.
You are on the right path and will achieve your objective with
patience and perseverance.

Know that with an open heart and mind anything can be
accomplished. Be grateful for what you have and more blessings
will flow into your life.

Affirmation
I am grateful and I am blessed.
With patience and perseverance I achieve my objective.
Life is an amazing journey.

The Infinite Space

"All children are artists. The problem is how to remain
an artist once he grows up."
– Pablo Picasso

You are experiencing a strong urge to express yourself creatively and the artist within you is emerging. Your inner artist is leading you to explore new pathways and ideas.

Expressing yourself creatively helps balance your emotions and improves your general wellbeing. This is a time to reconnect with your true self and the inner child who lives in the infinite space of your heart.

Ideas and inspirations are beginning to surface. Express them without censorship or judgement. You are limited only by what you think is impossible.

Affirmation
My creativity and potential are unlimited.
My inner child is my true essence.
I am balanced and whole.

Sea of Love

"Do not dwell in the past, nor dream of the future, but rather, concentrate the mind on the present moment."
– Buddha

Bless the past and embrace the present. Know that life is one eternal moment with no yesterdays, no tomorrows – there is just now.

Feelings of guilt or regret stem from a misconceived notion that if you had acted or chosen differently in the past, things would be different now. Yet in thinking this way you fail to see the positive effects your past actions and choices have had on both yourself and others. If you look closely and objectively you will see a positive side also. All of our experiences enrich us, and those around us in some way, regardless of what we do and don't do. Nothing is ever a mistake, for all serves its purpose.

Affirmation
I am the power of now.
I bless and release the past.
I accept all as it is.

Ideas in Action

Now is the time to turn your ideas into action and they will manifest endless blessings. Have a clear vision, set clear goals and take action, as an idea without action simply remains a latent concept. Ideas float around the world wide web of human consciousness until somebody picks them up and acts upon them to create something new.

Affirmation
I take action and my ideas come to life.
I have confidence and faith.
I have a clear vision of what it is I would love to create.

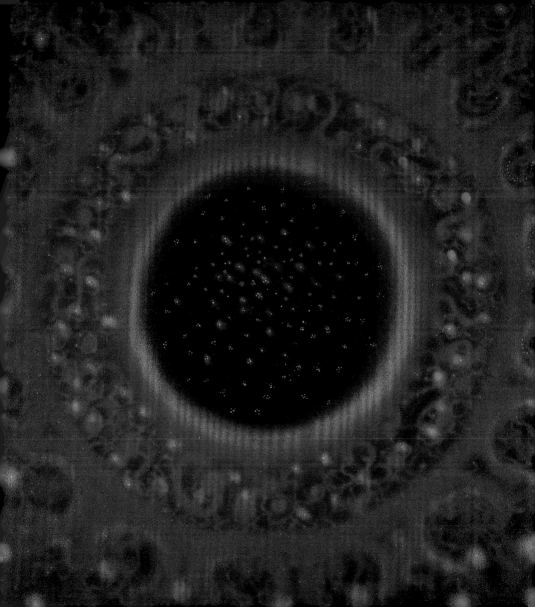

The Sacred Power

Doors that were previously closed now open. Pathways that were blocked now become clear. There is a sense of destiny about all that is unfolding. This is a blessed and fortunate time.

Be mindful of the sacred power you hold. Remain humble, strong and grounded. Feel your connection with Mother Earth beneath your feet.

Affirmation
I feel and honour the sacred power within me.
The way forward is clear.
All in my life unfolds with ease.

Emotions

Now is a time of healing and profound feelings, as a pool of suppressed emotions is expressed and released. It is safe to open your heart and trust. Allow all to come to the surface; empty yourself of everything. Vulnerability can become your greatest strength.

This is a time to heal old wounds, a time of great renewal, and deep and positive change. Towering waves of emotion become a tranquil sea of love. Light surrounds you and all is driven by the invisible wheel of love.

Affirmation
I open my heart and express all I feel.
I embrace the positive transformation occurring in my life.
I am an infinite ocean of light and love.

Spontaneous Creation

Your life force gives you unlimited potential to spontaneously create by tapping into the universal force of endless possibility. In this moment know that you are infinitely creative and endless creative potential fills your heart.

Every atom of your being, every molecule and particle of light is full of unlimited potential. Feel this force inside you; it is all around you and fills the world and Universe. Know that each breath you take is bursting with creativity.

Pay attention to impulses and ideas that come seemingly from nowhere. Trust your senses and be guided by them.

Affirmation
I am infinitely creative.
I am infinite potential.
I am a vast ocean of creativity and love.

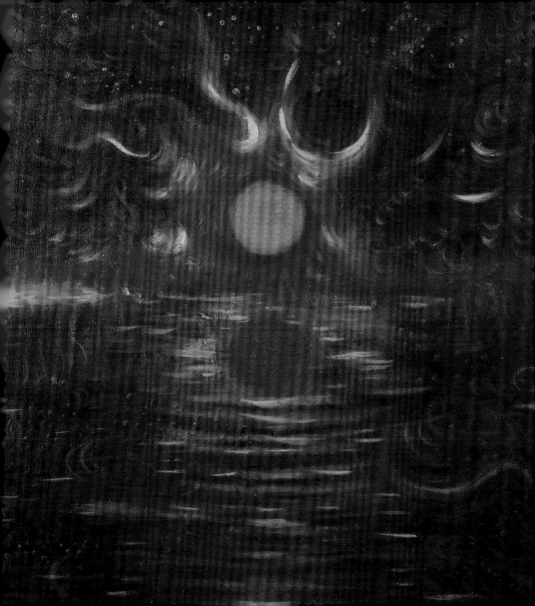

A Beautiful Soul

You are a beautiful soul, full of great wisdom and love. If you feel trapped, it is because you have helped create your own bondage. It is time to free yourself from the guilt and negative thoughts that are keeping you imprisoned.

Stop focusing on the negative and see all around you in a positive light. All is a matter of perception. Each time you catch yourself running a negative thought, stop and consciously replace that thought with a loving positive one. Continue to do this and the pattern will be broken, setting you free.

Affirmation
I am free.
I am love.
I am a beautiful soul.

Beloved

Through the magnetism of love you merge and love becomes
an all-embracing thought. A touch, a word, a glance, and love
unfolds its wings. Now is a season of love and romance. Two
beautiful souls within a diamond heart discovering the infinite
space of each other's soul.

Affirmation
I feel the infinite space of my soul and the soul of my beloved.
Love is infinite.
I am all that I am through love.

Life Unfolding

Change is on its way to you although it is not clear what she will bring until she arrives and reveals something new. Change is life unfolding and evolving as a new aspect of life is being born.

It is an unfathomable mystery, governed by a higher force that is beyond our knowing or control. Change is the essence of life that keeps things fresh. It unsettles and moves us along, it inspires and it brings new possibility.

The change that is coming is a blessing. Know that in her heart there is only love.

Affirmation
I trust that all is for my highest good.
I embrace change and the new blessings she brings.
I am safe and blessed by life.

Good Fortune

Good fortune flows to you like a mighty river bringing rich and beautiful experiences all interwoven in love. This is a spiritual awakening that illuminates both your physical and spiritual life. It is your next step on a journey towards enlightenment.

Affirmation
My heart and mind are illuminated.
Life is a colourful tapestry full of rich and rewarding experiences.
I am grateful for my good fortune and the blessings life brings.

Music of the Soul

An angel surrounds you with wings of light and is here to
remind you that there is more to life than your achievements and
possessions. She is here to help you reconnect with your inner
true self, which is unique, brilliant and sacred. Through this
reconnection the music of the soul is heard; it is a symphony that
fills the entire Universe.

Affirmation
I reconnect with my true nature.
I am a unique, brilliant and gifted soul.
This I that I am is eternal and infinitely beautiful.

Forgiveness

Holding on to past hurts and injustices keeps you imprisoned in your own pain. In forgiving you set a prisoner free, and that prisoner is you.

To forgive does not mean that you condone or approve of another's harmful actions. It just means that you are no longer willing to be that person's victim. Forgiving cuts the negative energetic ties that bind you to a painful past action. Set yourself free, because you are worth it.

Affirmation
I forgive and set myself free.
I forgive, honour, love and respect myself.
I release all past actions that have hurt me.
I am free.

Wisdom

True wisdom stands the test of time. When you do not compromise on the things you believe in, you honour and respect the divine being you are, and show great wisdom.

Through a series of unexpected but interrelated events, life is about to change for the better. In this moment something previously rejected is now accepted.

Affirmation
My inner wisdom stands the test of time.
My inner wisdom supports and guides me.
I accept, love and believe in myself.

Protective Presence

A great light shines upon you, illuminating your heart, mind and thoughts. All is clear and calm around you. You can move forward with confidence – you are protected by your destiny, which is waiting to be fulfilled.

Affirmation
I am peace.
I am clear like a crystal.
I move forward through life with confidence.

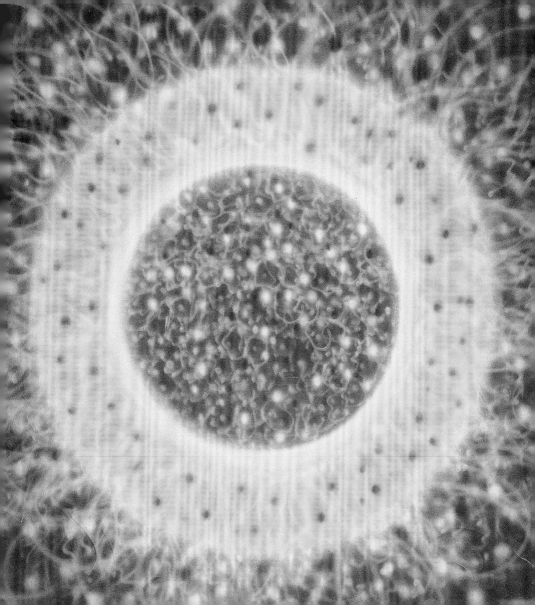

The Power of Now

The present is a result of the past. To change the future, we need to make different choices today.

Each and every moment holds great potential and is a miracle waiting to happen. Life is like a revolving door; when one door closes another automatically opens. It all depends on us, what we make of it, what we fill each moment with. Fill the present with love, and that is what you will receive in the future.

Affirmation
Today and every day I sow a seed of love.
I fill each moment with love and kindness.
Every moment is a miracle.

Question Your Beliefs

Take the time to examine your beliefs objectively; you may find that they are the source of most of your problems. Identify the ones that restrict you in any way as these keep you from experiencing greater joy.

Free yourself of all beliefs that no longer serve or support you. Pay particular attention to any beliefs that stem from fear. Do you really need these? If not, choose to replace them with loving ones emanating from your heart.

Affirmation
I release all beliefs that keep me from experiencing joy.
I release all beliefs that do not serve a positive purpose in my life.
Love guides me to peace and joy.

Seasons of the Heart

Accept the changing seasons of life. Know that all is unfolding as it should, in accordance with the will of your great soul.

Life is a benevolent force. Each season has its purpose and particular beauty, its challenges and blessings.

Each day is part of a divine evolution with each moment gathering precious memories to be embraced by the soul.

Affirmation
I embrace and love the changing seasons of my life.
Every moment and every day is a precious blessing.
All is held eternally in the heart of love.

Infinite Beauty

You are a beautiful soul, perfect just as you are, and there is nothing to fix.

The physical world is really spirit clothed in matter and from a spiritual perspective, anything you may achieve in this lifetime will pale into insignificance compared to the magnificence of what you already are.

What you are is a beautiful, creative and brilliant soul. Accept yourself as you are, and these qualities will soon become evident.

Affirmation

I love and accept every part of me as I am.
I am beautiful, brilliant and creative.
There is nothing I need to fix or change, all is perfect as it is.

Just Be You

You have much to offer the world by just being you, for you are unique and hold infinite love and wisdom.

Just be yourself, for there is nothing greater than you. There is no lesser or greater in each of us. Everyone is the power of God unfolding.

Butterflies are a powerful symbol for you at present; they are here to remind you about the 'power of you'. Remember this every time you see one for it is positive reinforcement that you are on the right path.

Affirmation
I offer a unique gift by just being me.
I am and all is God unfolding.
I am infinite wisdom and love.
I am always on the right path.

Timeless Earth

Connect with nature's healing energy. Feel her warmth and timeless love. All is in perfect harmony. Listen, feel, breathe the clean fresh air and clear your mind of all transient thoughts and concerns.

Rediscover life and its magic potential! Rediscover your own true self in nature's embrace.

Affirmation
I am spiritually connected to the earth.
Her healing power flows through me.
I am clear and calm.
I am inspired.

Living Energy

Thoughts and intentions are living energies that hold enormous power. They can build or destroy, give hope or take it away.

Positive thoughts and intentions create positive experiences while negative fear-based ones do the opposite. Lovingly focus on what your heart wants. Be clear about it. Know what you want and what you don't want.

If you want something to manifest in the physical world, you must first have that thought and intention inside you.

Affirmation
I create with positive loving thoughts.
My thoughts and intentions are clear.
I trust in the power of love to guide me.

The Wisdom of the Willow

The branches of a willow tree sway freely with the wind but its core remains strong with its roots firmly embedded in the earth. True wisdom is to be flexible and open, and at the same time, strong and firm. Your inner wisdom can see through appearances and connect with what is true. Sometimes, you stand firm in your truth but you must also remember that your truth is only true for you.

Life is constantly changing but your core essence remains unchanged since the dawn of time. Love and wisdom only grow stronger. Live and respond to all in your life through love, for in doing so you honour the spirit of all living things.

Affirmation
I listen to my inner wisdom.
I am guided by my truth
while respecting and honouring the truth of others.
Life is constantly changing
but love and wisdom only grow stronger.

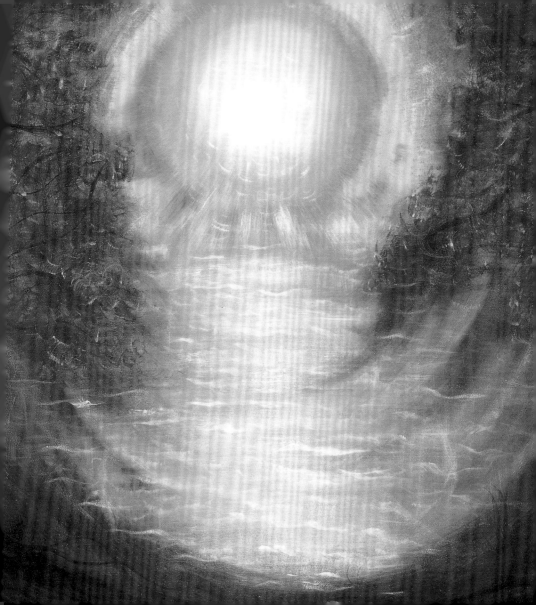

Creativity

Create, for it is in creation that you exist. Dare to be different; to make mistakes. In this world of dreams, that stems from the eternal heart of God, nothing will change the oneness that is. Go forth and be true to yourself for it is only through being true to you that you can be true to others.

Affirmation
I am unique and I dare to be different.
I create, for it is in creation that I exist.
I am one with life.

About the Artist & Author

My art is beyond words, it requires no thinking. There is nothing to understand, they are just colours, feelings and emotions that are felt in the heart. An open heart is all that is required. There is no particular meaning, each work may trigger something in the viewer or it may not. Each work is simply about love.

Toni Carmine Salerno is the author of many books, meditation recordings and oracle cards. He is also an artist who paints intuitively, creating works that are infused with a timeless sense of love. Born in Melbourne, Australia to Italian parents, the work of this internationally acclaimed self-taught artist and author and his publishing house, Blue Angel Publishing, continues to have a significant and positive effect on people's lives around the globe, connecting people and cultures through the universal language of love.

You can find out more by visiting **www.tonicarminesalerno.com** or **www.blueangelonline.com**

For more information on this
or any Blue Angel Publishing release,
please visit our website at:

www.blueangelonline.com